Darryl

by Brian Caswell

Illustrated by Phil Devine

Contents

Introduction	4
Chapter 1	7
Chapter 2	21
Chapter 3	31
Chapter 4	41

What *do* you do when the person who's meant to be your best friend tries to ruin your life?

Darryl

Paul has known Darryl all his life. They are supposed to be friends, but Paul doesn't trust Darryl. It's not surprising, because Darryl is always causing trouble — and pinning the blame on Paul. But one day, Darryl just goes too far ...

Paul

Darryl is no angel, but he never gets into trouble. He always lets someone else take the blame. Usually, that person is Paul. But when the truth finally comes out, Darryl finds out what it's like to be in *deep* trouble!

Paul tells the story ...

Chapter 1

I never did trust Darryl.

Everybody else did.

He was such a hero.

Football, basketball ... girls.

Even in Year 7 there were wild stories about Darryl James and girls. I didn't believe any of them, even though everyone else seemed to.

Of course, it wasn't *just* the girls. I mean, no one tells the truth about them. It was the little things. Things I knew he'd made up. Things that nobody else could know.

Nobody but me.

You see, we were meant to be friends. I guess we *were* friends. But a friend is supposed to stand by you. He isn't supposed to try and ruin your life.

We were the same age. Exactly. We were born on the same day, in the same hospital.

We'd lived in the same street all our lives.
And Mrs James was my mum's best friend.
Always had been.

Maybe he wasn't really trying to ruin my life. I guess he was just looking out for himself, as usual.

That was the thing that always worried me about him, even when we were friends. He never took the blame for things; he always found some way to get out of it.

Like when the football went through old Mrs Simon's window.

We always played football in the street. It's a dead-end and cars aren't a worry. But you just have to be a bit careful. Trouble was, Darryl got carried away.

His problem was, he always had to win. So he pushed a bit harder than everyone else, especially when he wasn't winning – which didn't happen very often.

Anyway, this time, for once, Terry Keegan and me were winning.

It was first to ten and we were up nine-seven.

You could see Darryl heating up.

He was throwing his elbows about ...

shouting at his team-mate Ronnie Jessup...

Straight into her sitting-room window.

Before the glass even hit the floor, he was off and running.

It was my football, and so I had to choose between asking for it back and losing it for good.

If I'd kicked his ball through the window, you could bet I'd be the one going to ask for it back. But not Darryl. And that was just like him.

As it turned out, Mrs Simon wasn't such a big problem after all.

Once I got up the nerve to knock on her door, the rest was easy.

The poor old lady was so lonely that the only punishment I got for smashing her front window was that I had to sit and talk to her while she fed me tea and chocolate biscuits.

Before I went, I asked her about the window, but she just smiled and said she was insured and that I was welcome to come back and talk any time. Which I did.

I didn't tell her who really smashed the window. There was no point. But that was always the way things worked with Darryl.

Chapter 2

I really should have seen it coming.

I walked into Darryl's house that morning – it was a Saturday, and we were supposed to be playing football – and his mum gave me this really strange look. Not her usual smile; more like she was studying me. Like I was a stranger. Then she turned to look out of the window.

She wasn't looking at me now, but I could hear her voice and it sounded ... strange. I stood there for a minute, but she wasn't going to say anything else, so I left.

Part of me wanted to run home, but part of me was scared. I didn't know why. I guess it was just that she had never sounded like that before and it worried me.

When I got home, my mum was waiting. She looked like someone had just punched her. For a minute, she just looked at me. Then she spoke.

"Paul ..." she said, then she stopped. Like she didn't know what to say next.

I didn't know what to say, either. I waited for her to go on. In the end, she did.

It was the only word I could make come out of my mouth.

They'd known me all my life. How could they think that?

"It was the money Darryl had been saving. To buy a computer. She said you were the only one who knew where he kept the money."

I guess that could have been true. Mrs James didn't let anyone except me into Darryl's bedroom.

And Darryl did show me the money once.

It was hidden at the bottom of his socks drawer. About fifty pounds. It was money he got for his birthday and Christmas. You know, that sort of thing.

But that didn't mean I took it! They should know that.

Mum was waiting. She wanted to hear what I had to say.

I wish I could say that everything was OK after that. It should have been, but it wasn't.

I could see that Mrs James didn't believe me. In one day, she'd gone from being like an aunty to acting like a stranger.

She really thought I'd done it.

Chapter 3

I saw Darryl at school on Monday.

I think he was waiting for it. He took me behind the bike shed.

So he started to explain.

"I didn't go to school on Thursday."

I knew that. I thought he was sick.

"Well, I wasn't sick ... I was with Tony Blake."

"Blake?"

I almost shouted it. Tony Blake was the biggest bully in the whole school. I'd warned Darryl about hanging out with him.

"We were at his house. Playing games on his brother's computer. And I ..." He stopped, like the memory scared him. "I knocked a glass of Coke over. Right into the computer."

He didn't need to say any more. I knew where the money had gone.

We had to get it fixed up before his brother got home. He would have killed us both.

The man at the shop fixed it up in a couple of hours, but I had to use the money I had saved up to pay him.

What could I say? I waited for him to go on.

"I couldn't tell the truth. If Tony gets caught skiving school again, he'll end up in real trouble. He told me what would happen if I talked."

I could guess!

"But why did you blame me?" I asked him the question, but I'd already guessed the answer.

"I didn't mean to. I couldn't tell my mum and dad what really happened, so when Mum found the money was gone, I just played dumb."

"Then she asked you who knew it was there." I carried on the story for him.

"Yeah. And I told her. I didn't think she'd think it was you who took it."

He looked sorry, but then, Darryl always looks sorry – after it's too late.

Look, it'll all die down soon. They can't prove you did anything . . .

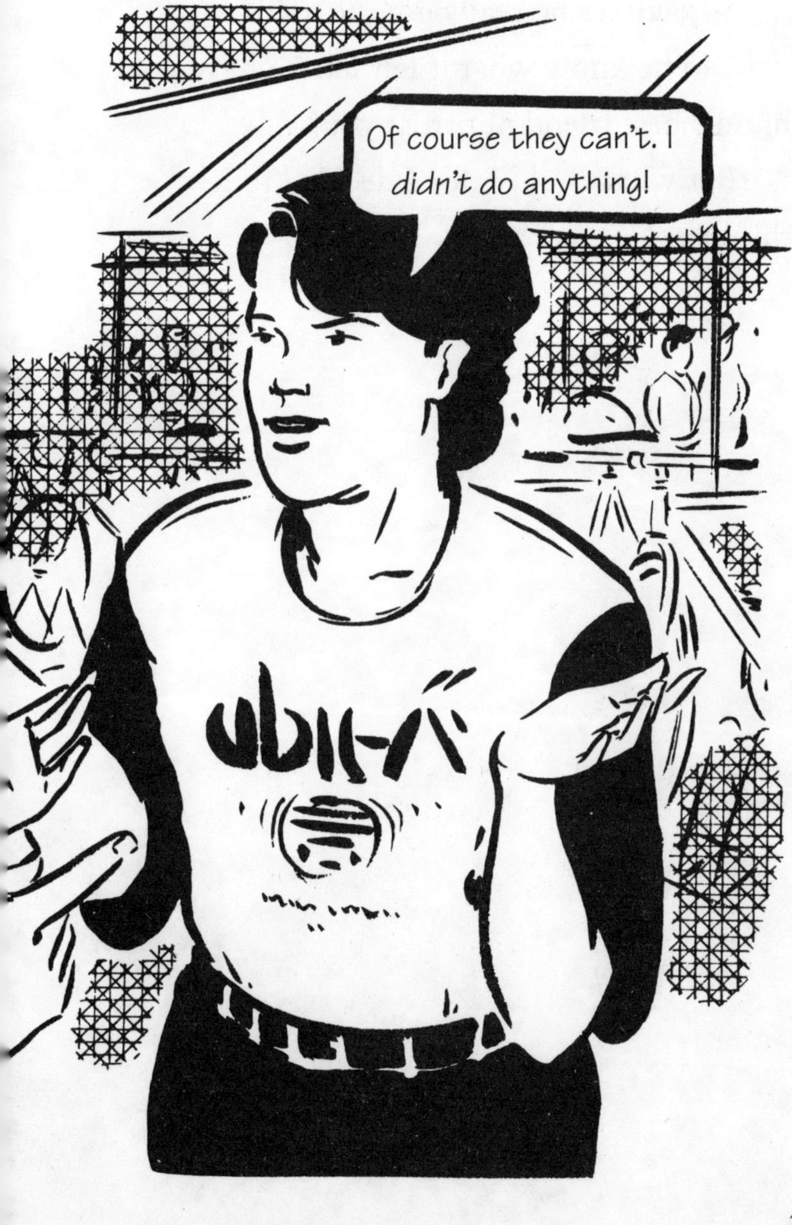
Of course they can't. I didn't do anything!

Sometimes he really got me mad.

Did he know what it felt like to have your mum's best friend not trust you?

But what could I do? I decided to let things go.

Chapter 4

And I would have let things go, too, if it wasn't for Sally Pitman and her mouth. She was as bad as her mother.

Mrs Pitman was the town gossip; she stuck her nose in everywhere. It seemed like it was her job to know everything about everyone, and she was very good at her job.

I never did find out how Sally knew about the money.

It must have been Darryl or his mother. I was too mad to ask him, and I didn't trust myself to get close enough to ask Sally. I'd probably have punched her.

Anyway, by lunchtime it was all around the school that I'd stolen the money.

Kids were looking at me and whispering.

Tony Blake was giving me warning looks.

And Darryl was staying out of my way.

I couldn't forgive Darryl for that.

In a few hours I'd been shut out. I was a criminal, and I hadn't done a thing!

Even a few of the teachers seemed to be looking at me funny.

Darryl, Tony and stupid Sally Pitman. I hated them. I hated what they'd done. I hated the fact that there was nothing I could do about it.

Who would believe me?

I had no proof. And anyway, I knew what that look from Tony Blake meant.

Shut up – or else!

If I wasn't in so much trouble already, I'd have skived school myself and gone home ...

I caught up with Darryl on the way home.

> Listen, you have to tell them. I know it's bad, but what about what's happening to me?

He just looked at me.

We were standing behind the fence in the park next to his house.

> I don't 'have' to do anything.

The way he said it, I knew – for the first time in our lives – that I didn't really know Darryl at all. "It's not my fault!" he said.

The way Darryl said it, I think he really meant it.

47

"Of course it's your fault!" I shouted at him, and pushed him against the fence. Hard.

Then Darryl's face went cold, like an animal's face. And his voice was cold too.

> You tell anyone, and you know what you'll get. Tony Blake will ...

He never finished what he was saying. Suddenly his mum stood up on the other side of the fence. She had her little gardening spade in her hand.

We hadn't seen her there.

Her voice was quiet when she spoke. But you could tell she was angry. Really angry.

And just what will he get? And what is it he's not allowed to tell anyone?

If she'd heard all of what we'd said, she knew already. But I think she was just getting warmed up.

I didn't stay to watch the rest. I didn't need to ...

Chapter 5

Mrs James said she was sorry for thinking I'd done what she thought I'd done, and I said it was all right.

She made Darryl say sorry too, but I told him to stuff it.

Tony Blake didn't get sent to a home or anything, but I think Darryl wished he had. Poor old Darryl keeps coming home with his shirt ripped and bruises in places where they don't show.

I don't go over to Darryl's house any more.

And neither does Tony Blake.

Except for yesterday, of course.

He didn't really go over. He only went as far as Darryl's front yard.

I was watching out of my bedroom window. It looks out over the street.

You see, Darryl had left his football outside.

Tony took it and kicked it through Sally Pitman's front window.

It's got Darryl's name written on it.

Now, if he wants it back, he'll have to go and ask for it.

I wonder if Mrs Pitman will be as nice to Darryl as old Mrs Simon was to me.

Somehow I don't think she will be.

Maybe I should tell someone what really happened. You know, just for old times' sake.

What would you do ... ?

TEEN LIFE, SET D

Darryl *by Brian Caswell*

Darryl seems so perfect. He stays out of trouble by making Paul take the blame for what he does. But Paul won't be pushed around for ever!

Missing on Holiday *by Pete Johnson*

Jo is in for a Holiday from Hell, stuck in a caravan with Mum, Dad and her little brother Craig. But then she meets Katie and Dan, and things start looking up ... for a while!

My Secret Love by Andy Brown *by Narinder Dhami*

Andy loves Beth. But how can he tell her? Every time he sees her, something goes wrong!

ANOTHER BOOK BY BRIAN CASWELL ...

Sweet Revenge

TEEN LIFE, SET C

Nick's had enough of Budgie's bullying, so he comes up with a plan to have his revenge. Sometimes, revenge can be *very* sweet!

ANOTHER BOOK YOU MIGHT ENJOY ...

Crush

by Jon Blake

TEEN LIFE, SET C

Ian's class have a wild time with their media studies project ... Somehow that video camera seems to land everyone in trouble – especially Ian!